Caleb's

Christmas Quest

Featuring Pigmuffin

By Dr. Evelyn Elliott Presley

Illustrated by Judith Gosse

Dedication

After publishing my debut children's book, Boo Thunder!, several readers asked about my next book. Truly, I had not considered authoring another book so soon after the first endeavor. However, out of the clear blue, a family tale about my beloved grandfather, Papa McClure, surfaced in my memory. At the same time, a picture of my great-grandson, Caleb, merged with my memory. I knew immediately that I had to immortalize the family story to honor my Papa and to welcome the newest member of my family. A purpose for writing was born.

I dedicate Caleb's Christmas Quest to my future generations and the loving memory of my special Papa McClure.

Magic and music fill the cozy cottage nestled at the North Pole. Caleb looks out his bedroom window and is delighted over the winter wonderland before him.

He holds his favorite toy, Pigmuffin, close to his heart.

"Look, Pigmuffin!" Caleb whispers as he points at the sky. "It's the North Star. Tonight, I make a special wish for a sister or brother."

With a big yawn, Caleb curls up in bed with Pigmuffin. Caleb's last thought before sleeping is of being a big brother. Caleb dreams of laughter, adventure, and love.

As the day begins, Caleb wakes up smiling.
The excitement of Christmas Eve swirls around him.

Caleb whispers to Pigmuffin, "Tomorrow is Christmas.
I hope I get my wish." Caleb jumps out of bed
and hurries downstairs with Pigmuffin.

"Ho, Ho, Ho!" laughs Santa with a wink. "Good morning, Caleb. We have something to tell you."

"Your Christmas wish is coming true," says Mama.

Papa says, "Your brother or sister is coming home with me tomorrow." Laughing, Caleb hugs his parents. "Wow! My Christmas wish is coming true."

"We have a mission for you," says Mama.
"Would you name the baby?"

"You want me to name the baby?" exclaims Caleb.
"It is an important task we know you can do,"
says Papa. "Yes, I will find the best name," says Caleb.

"That's my boy!" says Papa.

Caleb finishes his breakfast and puts on warm clothes.
He has a quest to complete. Carrying Pigmuffin,
Caleb's first stop is the North Pole gym.
The reindeer are working out.

"Hey guys," Caleb says. "Papa is bringing home a baby
tomorrow. What name would you give a baby?"

Dasher scratches his head. "How about Pepper?
We need something hot in the North Pole."

Comet jumps off the treadmill.
"I think the baby should be named Slick."

Cupid shakes his antlers.
"No, you need a stronger name like Bruno!"

Rudolph chuckles, "I'm the only one with a red nose. No one can use my name."

Caleb's surprise grows as the reindeer offer more suggestions. He quietly slips out, realizing that naming a baby is hard.

Caleb heads to the bustling toy workshop,
where the elves prepare Santa's sleigh.

"Hey, everyone!" Caleb calls out.
"Mama and Papa asked me to name
our new baby. Any ideas?"

The elves stop working to give
Caleb suggestions.

Sugarplum Mary says, "How about Twinkle Star if it's a girl and Scooter Pooter if it's a boy."

Bushy Evergreen chimes in, "I like Oakie Dokie and Daisy Maisy."

Alabaster Snowball offers, "I don't know about a girl's name, but Fred is a great name for a boy."

Caleb thanks the elves for their ideas. His shoulders slump. He begins to think the quest may be too hard.

Caleb goes to a quiet place to think. He wraps his arms around Pigmuffin. "Pigmuffin, what if I can't name the baby? I'm afraid I won't finish my mission."

Pigmuffin looks with love at Caleb. "You can do this. You are strong." Pigmuffin's quiet look reminds Caleb of how much his parents love and believe in him.

At lunchtime, Caleb returns to the cottage.

"How's it going?" asks Mama.

"It's tough finding a name," answers Caleb. "The elves and reindeer had some wild suggestions!"

Mama responds, "I can only imagine."

"But Mama," Caleb says,
"What if I pick the wrong name?"

Mama reassures him. "Caleb, you have wanted a
brother or sister for a long time. You have a good heart
and want to be a big brother. You can do it!"

Suddenly, there is a flurry of noise outside.
Caleb realizes Papa is leaving.

"Papa, wait," yells Caleb as he runs toward the sleigh.

"Ho! Ho! Ho!" says Santa. "Remember, Caleb, we chose
you for the mission because we believe in you."

Caleb's face lights up. "Papa, you taught me that I can do
anything if I believe in myself."

Papa winks and settles into the sleigh as he
and his merry reindeer disappear into the night.

Mama and Caleb go inside the warm cottage.

Mama suggests, "Look through the family photo book. One of our ancestors may have a good name."

"That's a great idea!" says Caleb.

Caleb looks at the family photos and sees Grandpa McClure's picture." That's it! I know the baby's name!"

That night in his room, Mama asks,
"Did the pictures give you any ideas?"

"Yes, I have the perfect name,"
responds Caleb with a smile.

Caleb falls asleep while Mama reads to him.

Caleb sits up in his bed. It's Christmas morning.

He grabs Pigmuffin and runs downstairs.

Papa is home and looks happy.

Mama is sitting in her rocking chair
with a smile on her face. Caleb hears a sound
coming from the baby on Mama's lap.

Mama says, "Caleb, come see our Christmas miracle."

Caleb peeks into the blanket and sees the sweetest baby.

"Meet your baby sister," announces Papa.

Mama asks, "What name have you chosen?"

As Caleb looks at his little sister,
he has doubts about the name he chose.

Mama notices Caleb's worried look.
She places a hand on his shoulder.

"Caleb, remember that your love for your sister is what's
important. What others think doesn't matter
because her big brother chose her name with love."

A smile covers Caleb's face.

"When I looked at the family photos,
I saw a picture of Mama's daddy, Grandpa McClure."

"I remembered Grandpa McClure's nickname for Papa.
Let's name her Sandy."

Mama and Papa exchange warm, loving glances.

"Caleb," says Papa, "We love the name Sandy. You have chosen a beautiful name that reflects our family's love. We are very proud of you."

The elves and reindeer jump with joy over the name.

Caleb's joyful laughter fills the room,
for he has finished his quest for a special name!

Caleb looks at his sister. "Sandy, I will teach you everything I know about the North Pole. As your big brother, I will protect and love you. We will have fun."

Snuggling in bed, Caleb squeezes Pigmuffin.
"I want to teach Sandy about believing in herself.
I want to be the best big brother!"

Dear Parents,

Caleb's Christmas Quest is a heartwarming tale about a sweet little boy who loves his family. He was thrilled to be entrusted with naming his baby sister. He was lucky to belong to a family that included him in responsible tasks. While Caleb was proud to be chosen, he was also concerned about being able to complete the request.

Caleb set off on a quest and had to learn how to keep going even when the answers were not where he looked. Such a journey isn't easy for any of us, especially a child. Like Caleb's parents, we all have a pivotal role in teaching a child to believe in themselves.

Learning to tackle a mission or quest and bring it to a positive end is a vital life skill. Completing missions as a child helps so that when one grows up, facing a daunting task does not result in avoidance.

A list of tools on the following pages provides suggestions to consider when teaching a child to believe in themselves. Additional ideas are available on my website: www.drepresley.com

Dr. Evelyn Elliott Presley

Helping Children to Believe in Themselves

Caleb's story reminds us that a family's love will help a child overcome the fear of failing, even when doubts arise, and the challenge seems too much. Love gives a child self-esteem and a belief that challenges can be positive. Teaching children to believe in themselves unlocks many possibilities for growth and a happy life.

Here are some ways that you, as a parent or caregiver, can help a child believe in themselves.

1.   Set Realistic Goals. Goals should be broken down into small, achievable steps. Small successes will build self-esteem.

2.   Emphasize problem-solving. Teach children how to solve problems on their own. There are several resources available that provide the tools for problem-solving. Research the best tools you can use to teach your child to problem-solve.

3.   Let them know that failure is part of life. Children must know that life has difficulties – victories and losses – that a child must expect to encounter. Knowing that setbacks will occur allows a child to accept what happens, so they are not unduly surprised. The key is for them not to give up.

4.   Teach a child to make age-appropriate decisions. This will assist the child to become independent. Decisions beyond age expectations may cause a child unnecessary stress. The child should be aware that the parent is the final decision maker.

5.   Avoid criticism. Do not get upset when a child makes a mistake. Do not scold or belittle them—especially in front of others.

Additional ideas are available at: www.drepresley.com

Acknowledgments

The readers of Boo Thunder!, my first book, have led me to publish another book. The positive feedback from children, parents, teachers, and caregivers has created a desire in my heart to provide books that will improve a child's life.

Judith Gosse, the illustrator, was adept at understanding my vision and putting it in beautiful pictures and colors that brought everything to life.

The BETA readers, Patricia Haddad, Linda Gradual, Dr. Gayle Swisher, Susan Rose, and Christina Metcalf gave their time and provided excellent feedback for improvements to my book. Once more, my mentor and editor, Betty Larrea, put me on the right path to start and complete my second book.

About the Author

Dr. Evelyn Elliott Presley has achieved a notable accomplishment by attaining a Doctoral Degree in Organizational Leadership, specializing in Conflict Resolution and Mediation. This educational journey has equipped her with a profound understanding to develop strategies that foster self-sufficiency, productivity, and growth across various age groups.

Dr. Evelyn Elliott Presley brings a wealth of knowledge to her endeavors with an extensive background as a campus president, academic dean, and educator within public and private educational contexts. Beyond daily operational management and regulatory compliance, her expertise encompasses creating tailored materials, formulating curricula, providing comprehensive faculty training, and facilitating dynamic virtual learning experiences.

At the core of Dr. Presley's mission is her passion and commitment to nurturing the leaders of tomorrow – children. She believes their empowerment hinges on confronting fears and nurturing confidence. Moreover, Dr. Presley is vital in aiding parents and caregivers in equipping children with the tools to cultivate a productive and happy life.

In January 2023, Dr. Presley marked a significant milestone by publishing her inaugural children's book, "Boo Thunder!" This literary achievement serves as a stepping-stone, as two more books are poised for publication within the year, promising to extend her mission of aiding and inspiring others.

Dr. Presley is an active community member who resides in Tarpon Springs, Florida, with her husband and cherished pets. Her involvements span diverse areas, including participation in the Tarpon Springs Writers and Authors Guild, the Windrush Bay Book Club, and the church choir.

About the Illustrator

Judith Gosse is an illustrator and designer who enjoyed a long and rewarding advertising career at J Walter Thompson and Bernard Hodes Group in the San Francisco Bay Area while raising two active, talented daughters. Judith moved to Washington, DC, where she worked as an Art Director and Illustrator for various DoD contractors, Fannie Mae, and the FAA for several years. In 2018, she left the fast-paced city life and now illustrates children's books in her Illinois studio.

"My mom insisted that my first word was pencil," she says. "I have lots of drawing tools now, and I am delighted to be doing exactly what I have always wanted to do – drawing for children."

43483418R00020